MW00777541

FINISHING LINE PRESS
www.finishinglinepress.com

FALCONS

For Sally — with thanks for past kindnesses! [illegible] 8/16/20

poems by

Michael H. Levin

3605 Tilden St. NW DC 20008-3124

Finishing Line Press
Georgetown, Kentucky

FALCONS

For Jean
Who nevertheless persists

ISBN 978-1-64662-232-0 First Edition

ACKNOWLEDGMENTS

Versions of some of these poems originally appeared as follows:

"A Banquet," in *District Lines III: An Anthology*
"April Again," in *Bethesda Poetry Festival Prize Poems*
"Anatolia" and "Speaking in Tongues," in *The Federal Poet*
"At Great Rock Bight," in *Dunes Review*
"Cam Ranh," in *Gargoyle Magazine 70*
"Cloaked Lamps" and "In the Crook of His Arm," in *Rat's Ass Review*
"Baghdad Nights," "City of Flowers," "In Sunlight, in a Beautiful Garden," and "Islas Encantadas," in *What Rough Beast*
"High Summer" and "Lost Wax Method," in *The Sixty-Four: Best Poets of 2018, An Anthology*
"Homecoming," in *Capitol Hill Rag*
"Junco in Junkyard," in *Apiary X* and *The Federal Poet*
"Martini Eves," in *What Rough Beast* and *The Spirit It Travels: An Anthology of Transcendent Poetry*
"Odyssey," in *Adirondack Review*
"Othello," in *Asides* (Shakespeare Theatre Company, Washington DC, March 2016)
"Scherzo," in *2019 Mizmor Anthology*
"Shield of Achilles," in *What Rough Beast* and *Capitol Hill Rag*
"Trinity," in *Spectral Lines: Poems about Scientists*

Publisher: Leah Maines
Editor: Christen Kincaid
Cover Art: Lesser Kestrel / shutterstock.com
Author Photo: Nora Jean Levin
Cover Design: Elizabeth Maines McCleavy

Printed in the USA on acid-free paper.
Order online: www.finishinglinepress.com
also available on amazon.com

Author inquiries and mail orders:
Finishing Line Press
P. O. Box 1626
Georgetown, Kentucky 40324
U. S. A.

Table of Contents

A BANQUET

(Finally, this wedding: Mayflower Hotel, July 2006)

Each course a metaphor: Ripe
melons' curled prosciutto tongues.
Rare meats, sliced succulent with
hunter sauce. The sun-struck contours of
a lush gold peach. Dark melted chocolate,
suave as the woodwind section
of a summer orchestra.

Oaths may be good, but currents shift
while set meals have a place for
each: even absence, even sorrow.
So square the circle, beat the drum—
our bridegroom and dear bride, so
long delayed, have come
to sound a spell as old as flutes

in glades. Father Sky
and Mother Earth, bind them in the dance
of realignment and rebirth.
Like hawks and fishes, let them
find their lives in motion and in
being still, and let them be
as wine in glass that glows translucently.

This table's our desire, our wish to them
for wonder—joint surprise.
So as they tender love and launch
their craft, please grant us
grace, and pause yourselves.
Alight; descend.
Partake.

ANATOLIA

(Homage to Omar Khayyam)

The goddess folds her golden wings
across the lintel of the sky
as light retreats from hummocked hills,
called inward by the muezzin's cry.

Bleached scents of climbing roses flow
on rivulets of air past low
domed tombs, reminders that the writs
of Mahmoud and of Suleiman

ran here. Reminders too, the slow-
paced arabesques of inlaid rooms,
the oriental glide in which
Roxana's viziers survive.

By dark possessed, in buried caves
and tumuli more ancient beings
persist, ceramic limbs clasped tight
or raised. To whom they prayed—all vows—

whatever sought—now smothered in
the drift of years: faith's sleight-of-hand
made manifest. All fades: all gods,
each columned hall and blue

pavilion. The lords of over-
lords are shards. Caught in a closing
noose of sight between arched entrances
and trapdoors of goodbye, we sift

such matters fruitlessly—small things
that perch, then fly. The goddess says:
Hold fast and sing, and sing again
beneath the Bowl of Night—lift high

the Cup; though answered only by an
echo; by the desert breeze's sigh.

APRIL AGAIN

blossoms brushed from bent limbs
in my hair, tangled with sweat
and pollen; the heat of first mowing.

Air tender and urgent
as moments we shared
on a night-lit stone porch above
turned Oxford meadows, when April

was dawn in Eden, first and new.
House wrens burble their down-song
screened by poplars.   Overhead, a
cardinal, flush with attitude,

follows my back and forth
curiously, scanning for seeds.

AT GREAT ROCK BIGHT

Ahead, white tide slaps shingle
with a sound of flesh on flesh,
a double line of footprints
on the wet tan beach
appearing molten briefly,
then erased.

Love is a craft
of necessary griefs.
The wound is present
when the tie is formed.
A strand of hair, a touch recalled;
the skiff that glancing back
we ride.

BAGHDAD NIGHTS

> *We gave them all our dreams—the magic carpet, the Arabian Nights. They used them for Disney films and brought us their tanks and their snipers.*
>
> *—Aziz Hassan, Iraqi poet (2016)*

Night shimmers along the Street of Books
over flat rooftops that promise relief
from crushing heat, disrupted
intermittently by bursts
of small-arms fire.

Aladdin's dream—that magic swirl of hope
where chance aligns and fortunes fall from trees,
once graspable in blue-tiled mosques
and arching passageways—is now consigned to
splintered palms, dry rubble piles.

His name was Allah-Din; but magic
comes obscured these days—small expectations
mixed with dust. What rises is uncertainty.
Each passage has gone blind. The nomad moon
hangs motionless, resigned.

CAM RANH

(Vietnam, 1970)

Guts on floor
not good for self-image,
so not like

x-rays in calm
black and white. What you
thought Body

turned inside
out like a glove who knew
you carried, sliding

down bunker
where concrete dust
drifts, heavy with silence

hearing the tramp of
blood in your ears, rising—rising—
coming on like dusk.

We're not books, though
we can be opened.
Don't ask

the purple sheen answers
naked as newborns. Insists
what we are

CITY LIGHTS

(1931: Chaplinesque)

She comes to the sill like sunbeams
hands light as butterflies.
He looks up, chipper and alien
as a squirrel.

It is a child's world,
this realm of rapt romance
and innocent, bruised expectations,
yearnings risky as eggs.

Others more powerful,
causes unguessable,
he stays small, duckwalks
down boulevards, pledges
his miniature selves.

Is the last take
when blind love
sees the tramp in us (that wound
of knowing—his eager patched

bag-trousered form
caught center stage,
frantic with fear)
a start or ending?

In the next revolution
past that courtyard arch
what will be kept— what discarded?
Flickering end-reel XOs
shadow laughter's afterglow.

CITY OF FLOWERS

(Firenze)

Serene behind its heart of beating stone
the city stretches and reclines in pleasing
narrow ocher curving lines; spreads its gray paws
upon the piazzas, haunches tucked against
precisely windowed and proportionate facades

turns—a glint of claws. Secreted daggers
at the Duomo's doors, Savonarola's
fierce dark face, edged as an axe,
still cut their ways below arcades
that run from weathered corner frescoes

past slit palace eyes, to the Campanile
lifting itself hand over hand in slender
colonnaded spurts of hope towards heaven.

What caused this nuclear outburst
we will never know, who talk
of grand dukes, Buonarotti, Fra Angelico

the power of limits and exploded laws
still volleys, vaulting passionate and hard
down arched percussive halls to where its dwarf
retainers troop—small shuffling bands
on tessellated floors.

CLOAKED LAMPS

[It's] a Republic, Madam—if you can keep it.
—Benjamin Franklin, 1787

What could I tell my mother,
that driven orphan who for all
her years refused to ride the
VWs that were
family business cars. She said
they made her gorge rise at the thought.
When friends went underground
she joined World Federalists.
I have still in a drawer
the olive-wreathed gold globe
she pinned to her lapels.

How outline on her webbed
Depression scars the ways
we mirror what brought Weimar down.
They claimed she could not grasp
how indirection may attain one's ends
but something tigerish infused her space.
She would not bear the easy
ways in which submission creeps
and secret places are where
life subsists. Do not abide,
she'd say, though fearful of the cost:

uncloak the Lady's lamp.
Stride forth. Persist.

EEL POND, SEPTEMBER

Who authored wonder
still delights to dance here. Salt and fresh water
swirl; marsh grass dips feathertops between.
Ponds coil their skeins while
gulls wheel over through a sky that repaints itself
in blinks of brightness.

Nature cannot sustain us
though my heart shifts strangely as the air puts on
its evening suit of lights and makes its first *paseo*
with that sequined cape.

The gods of awe still cast
a spell where ebb tides flow. Horizon burns. Your hand
dovetails with mine, smooth pear in ironwood,
on the return.

FALCONS

Let loose the falcons
let their jesses fly
their fierce wings cast no shadows
in a sunless sky

their yellow glares
click swiftly through
steep stoops (the dive, the deadly
tear), reflecting nothing

while absorbing all.
So actors float, then
swoop to seize small motions
that may body thought.

So artists fold their
wings and drop like stones
to pounce on transient
hues. So hunger fuels

those flights that yearn
to enter other lives
and see with different sight:
a risky game where hunters

can be prey and feathered
death is turnabout, fair
play. Reminders that when
streaking back towards lures

and resting hoods, we may
go missing; burn up
like the phoenix; or by chance
announced by ankle-bells

return.

HIGH SUMMER

It's all about passageways
isn't it? Rhizomes snaking through
loosened earth. Oaks thrusting taproots
towards buried streams. Striped bees buzzing
past petals crested with ladybugs,
dancing their codes of location.

Your eyes crinkled with mirth, it seemed,
we talked on flagstones dappled
with lichen and high-summer
murmurs, avoiding what once moved
between us. Or was that worry
I glimpsed between shadow and light?

Or moments when selves turned
transparent and each knew no
other, stopped between was and
will be? Shade has its own way of
seeing. Juggling with gravity
I'm here, looking at you. You're still
there, looking at me.

HOMECOMING

(Thanksgiving Eve: after 9-11)

Stars glint like change
in a purse snapped open;
the moon collars with ice. Time
floats in expectation
amazed again at its plunge
to winter night.

Now the
ingathering begins: a faint
drone of genes like damselflies
builds to a pulse, the throb
and aileron squeal of landings
drowned by silverware.

Pour out
the wine: at the long table
crowded with more than cousins
let us give thanks
for what we do not have—

split roofs, burnt towns,
a scrum of fleeing households
on the road. The slick
wet-lipped pornography
of vengeance—

accept instead
this warmth; this lavish
grace. This gleaming
incandescent silence.

HUNTING FLIES

(After Howl*)*

I saw the best dog of my generation
flash by the kitchen, snapping at flies.
White-furred and -plumed, ears back, he hurtled
silently through summer air against
the window where they looped and buzzed; fell flat.
Recovered then, fangs bared, and sprang again.
He never caught one; but in August light
reconstitutes himself—black lips

drawn, dark eyes narrowed in his predatory smile,
a lithe torpedo launched at targets out of reach.
I like to think we joined beneath the skin:
wolf brothers strung out loosely in a hunting line
where flies were sideshows, and the surge towards
a beyond was what electrified.

IN SUNLIGHT, IN A BEAUTIFUL GARDEN

(The Cloisters, Upper Manhattan, May)

This capital I'm gazing at
resolves into a cat-faced grin—
the Devil, just swallowed a soul.
His thin smile spans a chalky block
where frog-eyed minions prod roped sinners
towards roaring flames of Hell.
One's upside down—kicked shanks trail
round the corner, ready to be hurled.

Meanwhile a medieval square of
daffodils and gentians bobs
softly in a breeze that brushes
their living carpet, sighing
through potted orange trees
and sun-splashed colonnades.

Ease, buttressed by sandstone
certainty: a riot of petaled
flares and stars where terrors
of Below are checked by chiseled
images—its snarling beasts
faith-tamed. Watching streaked sparrows

twitter down to sip at fountains
salvaged from ruined convents at Bonnefont
or Cux, I finish off my baguette crust
and contemplate grave courtesies
that nodding lavender and rose
still offer up in stained-glass hues,
defying more unhallowed times
upon their sward of grass.

IN THE CROOK OF HIS ARM

I'm held, straddling his lanky thigh,
wrapped in a double-breasted coat
and sweater that enlarge
my toddler frame.
We're on a bench, outside. He wears
a regulation tie,
the khaki G.I. shirt that
still hangs in my back-of-closet
and my mind, too fragile now
to take down or to wear. It seems
I've just been jounced on his big knee:
my breathless glance hints
recent glee. Remembered clip-clops
can't be traced to this March scene.
They rise instead from hours
I bounced my own small sons,
blurred imprints from a different time.

Why does this picture
move me so? Perhaps it's his
enchanted gaze, the smile
of one who seldom smiled in
later days. Perhaps it's (looking back)
how young he seems: broad face aligned
precisely with my tiny shoulder-edge;
the tendoned hand that steadies me,
his red-gold hair slicked sideways
from a part I don't recall. There are
no wrinkles here; no chasms carved
by worry or despair. No slow
retreat beneath the pressures
of disease and fear. I want to
twist round and return his grin
and state at last his many gifts
that went unsaid, and say that no one

is to blame for afterwards;
and—once more sheltered from the
universe—to nestle in.

ISLAS ENCANTADAS

(In Darwin's Galapagos)

A ghost volcanic blast
unlocks the surface of a white-capped
dolphin sea. Two hundred necklaced islets
rise in time-lapsed spree

uplifted by a molten platform
on the ocean floor—erupt, go dark,
collapse upon themselves; acquire
green mantles and new bursts of seeds

appear to die then leap to life again,
repeated resurrections born of
warm spring rains.

Sailing due east in geologic time
they make perhaps an inch a year
towards trenched submersion while new
cones rear up behind them

emblems of an earth alive.
Those first ashore (a churchly mission
bearing crosses) thought surely they had
entered hell: sheer lava cliffs, dark

glistening spews, crevasse-cut flats
crawling with dragons,
crimson crabs, huge
tortoises that tractored
sandy trails. They had keen sight
for faith, but none for miracles:
slate-colored lizards that sneezed salt

to cleanse their blood; tall dandelion trees
that sent trapped water down to shade below;
balloon-necked birds with razor bills
that floated near their cowls—all blindly

or with motions meant to exorcise
flew by. Blinkered by unexamined choice
they saw masked evil in creatures

lighting on one's hand—malevolence
in flowers turned yellow, adapted to
the menu of the Islands' bee.
Between the fumaroles, a differently

invested eye might just have glimpsed
the symphony of rise and fall
embodied in these views—
in finches custom-tailored

to their missions in such
merciless terrain or tufa cauldrons
simmering with life, all dancing

to a metronome whose ticks
dwarf human minds. Still under orthodox attack—
reflexive horror at a streaming
which admits no charity and shows

a face more like remorseless
storm surge than accustomed gods—
that vision rests on stepwise method
shaken free of rote. Conditional

as turtle eggs or seal pups
we reprise his browned
laconic notes.

JUNCO IN JUNKYARD

Obsidian-eyed, she wheels
and flits past pitted bumpers
through the monotone of engine blocks
and peeling limousines; lights pertly,
preens, then on a delicate flexed wing
sideslips precisely like a
seamstress threading a needle.
A breath; she banks; is gone.

So others who seem weathered gray
may strike a second's rustproof
pose, or flash an instant's covert
whites. It's accidental grace
that gleams—reprising
what's been lost, what won.

LATER,

I'll cry for you
but not now, with house wrens
returned to their snow-split box
above the new daffodils, burbling
their five-note code of starts
and renewals. Our red-nailed
crepe myrtle sways to a kite breeze,
shimmies in afternoon light.

Separate—the root condition:
Odysseus' long yearning. Yet
yellow heads dance while the ghost
of your body surrounds me, rich
as a ploughed field; its hollows
loamy and grooved.

LOST WAX METHOD

The childless house we moved to
in the Fifties was gummed with Christmas
firs, ripe apples, squirrels and fox cubs,
two-tooth Gerber grins: stickers, pressed on
bare walls. Some crazed wife leaving marks,
the agent said.

Our carpenter re-stained scratched floors,
replaced split sway-backed banisters
with sleek wrought iron. Smooth plaster,
sky-blue wallpaper appeared.
At sixteen I could sense returning
warmth, the heat

of new-glazed hearths transforming
troubled rooms; but not that shelters can
be molds where griefs of former occupants
adhere, turn liquid, trickle out.
Refurbishing did not prevent
our father's

golden glance descending into
corridors of gloom; our mother
hammering her plumb-line course
through shrinking doors. Did not preserve
their space of shared beneficence
and pain

I think I witnessed once, before
its frame clamped shut. They each died waiting:
she for unvarnished ends to take
effect; he at our corner stop for a
symbolic bus—mad barren woman
pacing

the backdrop who knew more than
well-groomed sons suspect, pushing
her thumbs against flat fate. Lost
wax: scorched residues I bear
in runnels of spilled chances,
wintry dreams

of unroofed days.

MARTINI EVES

I think more now of those dead:

the slim sax-playing therapist with
his perceptive spouse—my parents'
neighbors in late life and nearby graves

the black-caped architect,
wax-moustached and just north of crazed
by standards of the day, who built
curved structures and would blast walls
unpredictably with baritones

ex-Reds who strolled in trailing wives near
twice their size, to wander through my pre-teen
home among attentive brokers,
G-men, flacks for unknown causes
and mysterious mills, beside the limber
couple who learnt cha-cha first
and taught them all.

Martini eves where I, half up the stairs,
watched elders in pressed suits and cocktail gowns
put drinks and cigarettes aside to twirl
across our blue pile rug in Latin time
to spinning forty-fives. Just folks: a
comfortable group ascending on a
Fifties tide, as though in pantomime.

Yet in that crowd were some who carried hunger
far past seventh grade, and some who worked three jobs
to grasp degrees, and veterans of the Bulge or
Lawyers Guild; and some who proud as kings
refused to testify.
                                        Dance nights, astonishing
and rare, when I joined awkwardly the slinky
glides of those who carved their profiles, deeper
than they knew, in smoky air.

METAMORPHOSES

Then we were old.
It happened suddenly
while we were looking back:
an easy stroll displaced
by joints and spotted
epiderms. Touch was
our parlance; now words sparse
as hairs suffice. Where
did that limberness go,
the grace so comfortably assumed?
Routines cross quietly,
our offspring mortised into other lives
or hunkered down in basements
still unlaunched.

Unless there be
a hunger of the mind, all hungers
drift and dessicate—balloons loosed
into clouds. What stays are sprigged bouquets
of jonquils or draft stanzas that I
bring you, hoisted with effort
up strange heightened stairs. Mementos
of what's shared though half forgotten.
Vessels of surprised small joy.

ODA ENSALADA

(After Neruda)

O vegetables in lapis bowl
so finely clothed in dinner dress
of seasoned oil— your crispy lobes
of green and gold suggest refrains,
though still you seem too shy to speak.

I'll give you voices. Purple onion
take this sax—its burred long
tones bring edge to match your bite;
carrots, the sunset glow of cello
notes, plaited in warm

continuo. Cucumbral shade
bright radish too, can have your say
with silver flutes whose light glissades
will punctuate the cool tossed mix.
Yet fennel needs a subtler touch:

smoky and feathered at the top
descending through pearl mottled stalks
to sweet elusive anise crunch—
only massed French horns will do.
Roast beets take on vermilion tones

from oven heat and rounded growth
in loam—wood xylophones
perhaps, or bongos syncopated
with a lagging salsa beat.

In salad can be found
a world: rhythms of root and bulb
and leaf, embraided in a single line,
preserved pre-glacial forage times.

That score has faded; yet a fragment
of its tune remains. From corners
of the room Neanderthals peer out,
while I, unheeding, dine.

ODYSSEY

(In Menemsha)

Crafty Odysseus knew that time is this soft wind
from the east, falling and falling across our silvered
lawn, dropping sweet moisture where dim rainbow doves emerge:
endless and sudden. He stopped it with a spear
to bring his splintered family back—a clever trick,
but its sequel is troubled: the aging hero,
heavy with honors and the pull of old journeys,
steps off an Ithacan cliff.

Sorcery subtle as weather or unfolding smoke,
risky as upland boars, the traveling pitchman found.
Corrupt displacement was the rule, each healthy urge turned
monstrous,
upside down. And who am I to judge that pilgrim's lies, swung
against lies to clear his own path home?
So you in your time and me in mine, this quiet space
a charm against unquiet days, I track dove murmurs in the
roosting oaks, and put my boots

up on the rail; and simplify.

OTHELLO

(Director's Notes)

Ruin; *ruin*—beneath each spangled chair,
behind plush tapestries, along curved
balustrades and blinding white piazzas—
glides on, unwinding to its own cold beat,
more painful because most domestic.
Of all Plays rooted in families
the one most battened there, constricting
to hands round a dear bride's throat.

What score notates the music that "the
thick-lips" speaks? The General is his
language: a filigree of dew-rust,
anthropophagi, and camels
tethered under alien skies. A net
of scars from hardships passed, bleak exile,
slashing battles won. The Moor's a Martian—
dropped in the middle of a courtly snare,

his warlike core unused to indirection
or suspended judgment, unskilled at nuance
or with those who would draw ill upon
their world. Unlearned in pure negation
without cause. So, team: the questions are
why evil is, if trust can be, and where
it should be placed. My job's not answers
but to highlight starkly as the wheel

rolls on—yours, to stay innocent
despite that ache nearby the heart
until the claw-snap of the end, the awful
thunderclap of that reversing close.

SCHERZO

(Anna Burstein-Bieler, Pianist, 1908-2003)

1. Ernst (1926)

When I first came to Leipzig,
just eighteen, he shared
a house I played at for my
weekly meal. He had a sweet violin
as we moved easily
through Mozart chamber parts.

His scar from service at the Front
would glisten when he looked at me.

First love's a rush where everything
contracts to hands and eyes. I'm still
amazed I locked my door.
In four years I convinced myself
that I was over him.

2. The Conservatory (1926-1929)

They came from Russia Queensland
South America, the prodigies
and floods of acolytes.
My master class
was *something terrible* in all
respects: to play a new piece
every week, with all that
competition looking on.

The first three months
I overworked my right.
The next three months
that arm was in a sling.

I practiced with my left,
so clumsily. But learned
it's the foundation for the rest.

3. Johanna-Park (1935)

With my first-born we lived
on König-Johann-Strasse.
Our neighbor had
a son that age. Lotte
was full of life. Her organ-playing
brother left for Paris by this time.
We'd push our strollers to the Park
and let the *kinder* romp.

I walked that Park four decades on
and still could hear her voice.

4. Halina (1931-1999)

She was a wild girl, that one.
To her no normal rules applied.
They had a marriage open
as her creed. I ask no questions
or does he, she said. Why cast
a stone that hits you in the mouth?

She wrestled me to play those
two-piano concerts for the
Culture Bund. I didn't want
my name so high on Nazi lists.
You'd disrespect Johannes Brahms
from fear? she hissed—
that's what they want. Reviewers

said I stole the show.

Through exiles and returns and
all the detours of survival
by design and guile and all the
losses of the War and post-War years
we're still each other's witnesses,
still friends.

SCORCHED BRONZE

(For Travis Tuck, Vane Sculptor, 1943-2002)

It's not in sheet brass that the strength resides
or hammered copper or scorched bronze's sheen.
Fierce will makes form and function coincide.

Raked to the breeze your anvilled shapes still ride,
forever fleet of wind machines.
Yet not in metal does their power reside.

Making's an act of patricide,
honoring fathers as we pick them clean.
A hunger splits off form from function to devise.

Behind your gaze, a steel divide:
those who struck true from those who temporized.
It's not in metal that strength long resides.

Living's a slippery stepwise slide,
disjointed parts unless fire intervene.
Iron will drives form and function to elide.

Death is a small blue flame that reifies.
I saw you forge and know what slipped between.
It's not in metal that strength long resides.
Slow passion's where our legacies abide.

SHIELD OF ACHILLES

(After Auden, 1952)

Peering over his shoulder
the goddess of love in all her melting forms
sees no glad world of giving
molded there, no inlaid scenes of sacrifice
or service or of modest
calm obeisance to acknowledged modes
of conduct, much less law. Abrading
the bronze surface as it sets, corrosive pride
coils, pocking the arc
of honor, clouding blue air.

Absorbing what her spouse has made
she shudders, seeming for the moment older:
emblazoned at the center
of the metal field a bulky figure squats,
sniffing the sluggish breeze for prey that doubt
or might decline to play his
cat-game, batted publicly
from paw to paw.

Degraded from foundations
out, the house of freedom trembles towards the pit,
unmoored by shouted or implicit
threats infesting it.
The bulwarks sought do not appear,
submerged in self-regarding greed
or fear. The Botticelli
gaze turns gray. Her jealous hairy
husband sneers triumphantly
then limps away.

SPEAKING IN TONGUES

(Beginning with a line by Marjorie Sadin)

The river is speaking in Yiddish:
it pushes along, throwing up hands
in Levantine gestures, muttering
fishmonger curses under its breath.
A turnip should grow in your belly,
it says. *Put your butt on the table*
meaning talk straight, no fancy words here.

Now it's high-collared Russian—opaque
and moody, sideslipping rocks
like live carp flopped from carts. *Bread,*
it whispers through a cut overhung
by black pines shedding needles.
Eat bread and salt, and speak what is truth.

Surging towards delta, it shape-shifts to
Balkan—dividing, submerging; raising
islands from voids. *Beware,* it implies,
proud as Cossacks on stallions:
unreasoned destruction is mine to unsheathe.

My grandmother, dying, said, *Who will*
now save me. Though eighty years gone then
her tones were Carpathian, their timbre
shawled end-notes of doom.

My father age thirteen sang crabbed
Aramaic for part of the service
declaring him grown. Those tropes
still resounded when we laid him down.

Silted with pasts, we channel
banked ways—half-translated phrases
that echo lost days.

TRINITY

(Journada del Muerto New Mexico, 16 July 1945)

Let not this heat dispirit me
that streams so fierce it blisters skin
past gaps which cover miles,
or blinding light that turns the
blue hills white; but then the wind
a dragon's breath that flattens scrub
and banshees on as though to
never end—but then a growl
that rumbles like the heaving earth
might rise, cascading in an
angry swirl to coffin
up scorched observation posts.

Please god, the work was fire: six
years of sweated midnight math,
precision grinding, shouted
disagreements while our soup
or scrambled eggs grew cold. The
path Prometheus took, made new.
What batters now no witness
on this Dead Man's Trail dare say.
Ears plugged, we brace with stunned
relief against the booming
air. Exhale, and glance away.

Mike Levin has been writing creatively all his adult life, legal deadlines notwithstanding. He has degrees from the University of Pennsylvania, Harvard Law School, and Oxford University (U.K.), where his M.Litt. dissertation focused on how the tragic vision is implemented by dynamic theatrical forms. Pursued by a Vietnam-era draft board, he declined playwriting fellowships to Carnegie and Yale Drama Schools, likely saving American theater. He has published poems in two chapbooks, several anthologies and dozens of periodicals, and has received poetry and feature journalism awards. His collections *Watered Colors* and *Man Overboard* were named Best Poetry Books for May 2014 and December 2018 by *Washington Independent Review of Books.*

Before private practice Mike served as an appellate lawyer and executive in several federal agencies; in the Carter White House as Deputy Director of a Cabinet-level OSHA Reform Task Force; and as legislative aide to former Rep. Andrew Maguire (D-NJ) and Senate Judiciary Committee aide to the late Sen Edward M. Kennedy (D-MA). In 1982 he was awarded the U.S. Environmental Protection Agency's Gold Medal for Exceptional Service. An environmental lawyer and solar energy developer, he also is principal in a renewable-energy investment firm and Contributing Editor to *BioCycle Magazine*. He has been listed in *Who's Who in American Law, Who's Who in Business and Finance,* and *Who's Who in the World.*

CPSIA information can be obtained
at www.ICGtesting.com
Printed in the USA
JSHW020442040720
6507JS00002B/193